A W...
with Words

Contents

Features

WORD BUILDER

Which word is used to describe a person who can speak several languages? Find out on page 11.

Do you think it would be helpful if everyone spoke the same language? Check out **A Universal Language** on page 12.

WHAT'S YOUR OPINION?

PROFILE

Who wrote a play about accents? Turn to **A Master of Words** on page 15 to find out.

Are you a whizz at text messaging? Try decoding one of the newest forms of language on page 23.

FACT FINDER

SITESEEING • ART & ENTERTAINMENT

When did crossword puzzles begin?

Visit www.rigbyinfoquest.com
for more about LANGUAGE.

Talk, Talk, Talk

Language is one of the most important differences between humans and other animals. All animals are able to communicate with each other using noises, signals, and movements. Only humans, however, have true language.

Every day, we use language when we talk, sing, and write. We have developed technology such as telephones and computers that allow us to communicate with people far away. We also have languages especially for people who have difficulty seeing or hearing. We rely on communication so much, you could say that language makes the world go around!

Parrots are highly intelligent birds that can be trained to repeat words, but they do not have true language. Few parrots can use words to express feelings, and their language is learned, not **instinctive.**

Throughout this book, keep a lookout for words meaning "hello" and marked with *. How many of the languages do you recognize?

** **Hello**

Sign language is used by people who are deaf or have hearing impairments and by others communicating with them. It is a language made up of gestures and hand symbols. Ideas and concepts can be expressed through gestures, or words can be spelled out using the finger alphabet.

h

e

l

l

o

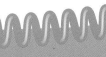

Sounds Like Speech

Spoken, or **oral**, language is made up of a collection of special sounds we make to represent people, objects, actions, numbers, colors, and feelings. We use our brains to remember words, put them in the correct order, and make our **larynx** produce the correct sounds. The story of speech does not end there, however. We use our jaws, tongue, cheeks, and lips to shape the sounds into words.

Can you figure out the sounds the boy in the pictures below is making? Match the sounds *aaah, eeee, oooh, mmmm* to the pictures.

1

2

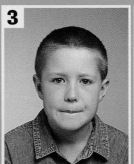

3

4

Answers: aaah=4, eeee=1, oooh=2, mmmm=3

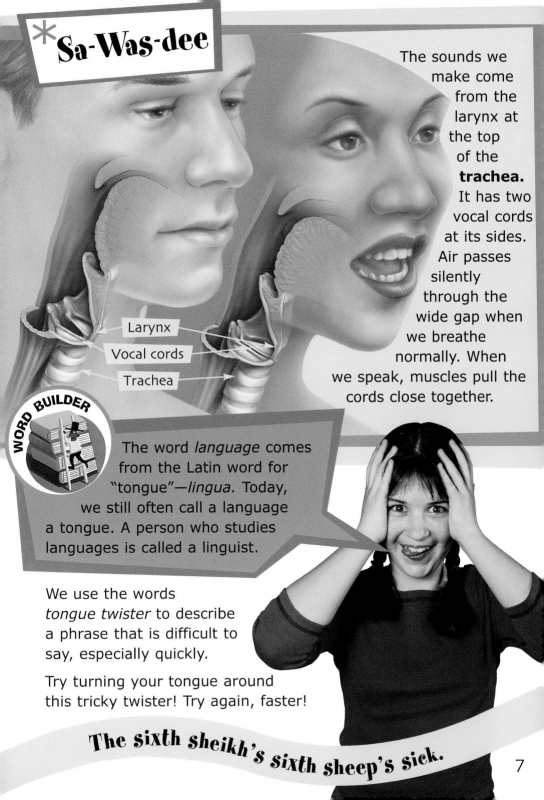

*Sa-Was-dee

The sounds we make come from the larynx at the top of the **trachea.** It has two vocal cords at its sides. Air passes silently through the wide gap when we breathe normally. When we speak, muscles pull the cords close together.

Larynx
Vocal cords
Trachea

WORD BUILDER

The word *language* comes from the Latin word for "tongue"—*lingua.* Today, we still often call a language a tongue. A person who studies languages is called a linguist.

We use the words *tongue twister* to describe a phrase that is difficult to say, especially quickly.

Try turning your tongue around this tricky twister! Try again, faster!

The sixth sheikh's sixth sheep's sick.

Learning Language

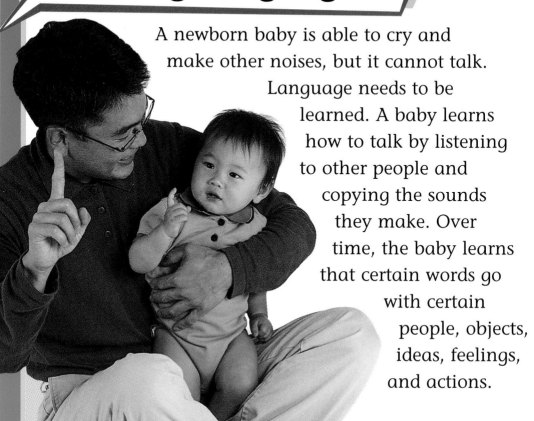

A newborn baby is able to cry and make other noises, but it cannot talk. Language needs to be learned. A baby learns how to talk by listening to other people and copying the sounds they make. Over time, the baby learns that certain words go with certain people, objects, ideas, feelings, and actions.

Children's Language Development

Average Age	6 months	1 year	1 ½ years
Language Skills	Babbling	A few words such as *Mama*	Some nouns, but no phrases

Experts have found that all over the world and in every language, parents talk to their babies and toddlers the same way. They use a high-pitched, repetitive, singsong voice that helps a baby learn the connections between words and objects. This special way of talking is called parentese.

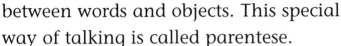

* **Hola**

Since the 1960s, there have been several experiments in teaching various sign languages to chimpanzees and gorillas. Some chimpanzees, such as Panibasha (shown left), have matched symbols to objects. However, they have not developed true language.

2 years	2 ½ years	3 years	4 years
More than 50 words, short phrases	Longer phrases, short sentences	Around 1,000 words, longer sentences	Close to basic adult speech

A World of Words

Everybody uses language, but not all language is the same. There are about 6,000 different languages spoken in the world today. Some languages are spoken only in certain areas by small groups of a few hundred or a few thousand people. Other languages are spoken by millions of people around the world.

Languages are classified into groups called families. Each language in a family is similar because it developed from the same original language, called a parent language. As groups of people moved away from each other, the language of each group changed. Over hundreds of years, these changes became so great that the groups could no longer understand each others' language.

Simple words are often quite similar in a language family. The English word *mother* is *mata* in Sanskrit, *meter* in Greek, *mater* in Latin, *madre* in Spanish, *mutter* in German, and *mat'* in Russian.

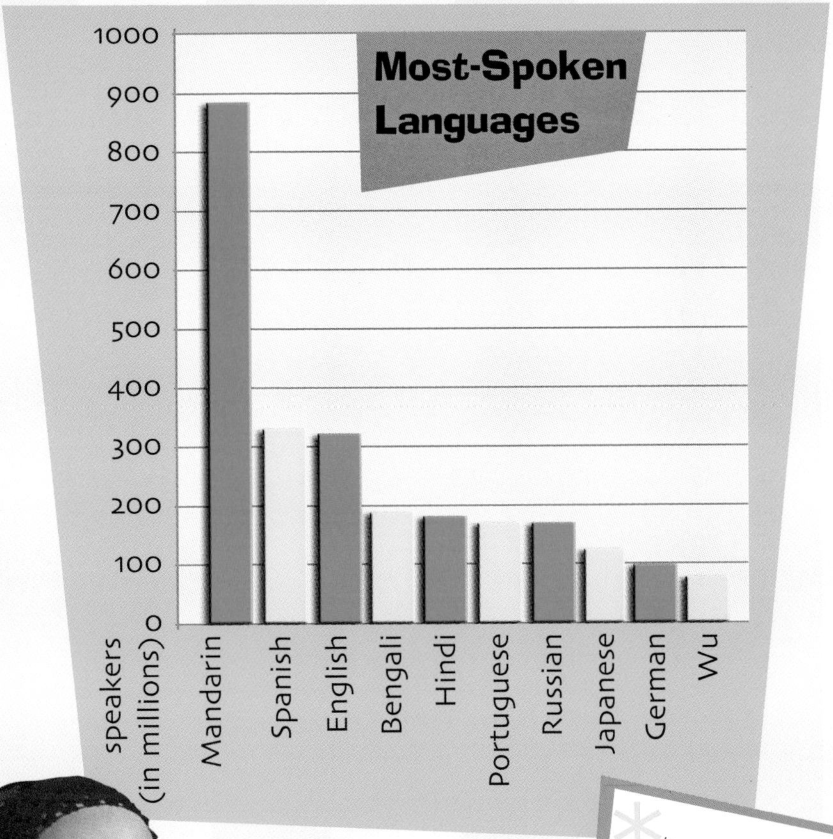
Most-Spoken Languages
1000
900
800
700
600
500
400
300
200
100
0
speakers (in millions)
Mandarin
Spanish
English
Bengali
Hindi
Portuguese
Russian
Japanese
German
Wu

***Tena koe**

WORD BUILDER

People who speak only one language are described as *monolingual.* Those who speak two languages are described as *bilingual.* People who can speak several languages are described as *multilingual.*

My Words, Your Words

The trouble with having so many different languages is that it makes communication difficult. Since the 1600s, people have been working on the idea of a universal language that everyone could speak and understand. More than two hundred universal languages have been invented since that time.

WHAT'S YOUR OPINION?

A Universal Language

The idea of a universal language is fine, but it would be impossible to teach it to everyone. Besides, why *should* everyone speak the same language? My language is an important part of who I am, and I don't want to lose it.

I think a universal language is a great idea. It would help bring the world's people together. If people all spoke the same language, there might even be less war.

The most successful of these artificial languages has been Esperanto. It was developed in 1887 by a Polish doctor to allow people who speak different native languages to communicate. Esperanto has a very simple structure and is four times easier to learn than any other language. Since its creation, more than 10 million people have learned Esperanto. Currently, there are about 2 million Esperanto speakers.

* **Ha lo**

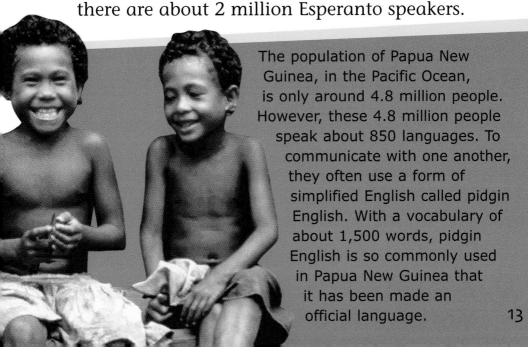

The population of Papua New Guinea, in the Pacific Ocean, is only around 4.8 million people. However, these 4.8 million people speak about 850 languages. To communicate with one another, they often use a form of simplified English called pidgin English. With a vocabulary of about 1,500 words, pidgin English is so commonly used in Papua New Guinea that it has been made an official language.

I Like To-mah-to . . .

Differences in the way words are pronounced, used, or spelled are common. The English language varies greatly across the country of England, and even more across the world. You can often tell where people come from by listening to them speak. Differences in **dialect** and **accent** may come about due to location, social rank, tradition, education, age, and occupation.

One famous English dialect is cockney. Speakers of cockney are said to be born within hearing distance of the bells of St. Mary Le Bow, a church in the city of London.

You say eether and I say eyether,
You say neether and I say nyther;
Eether, eyether, neether, nyther—
Let's call the whole thing off!

You like potato and I like po-tah-to,
You like tomato and I like to-mah-to;
Potato, po-tah-to, tomato, to-mah-to—
Let's call the whole thing off!

From the song "Let's Call the Whole Thing Off" by Fred Astaire and Ginger Rogers

*Jambo

A Master of Words

George Bernard Shaw (1856–1950) was one of the most famous writers of the 1900s. This British author wrote over fifty plays and many essays, and he was awarded the Nobel prize for literature in 1925. Shaw's writing was often filled with wisdom and wit, or humor.

One of Shaw's most famous plays, *Pygmalion*, was about how accents are often foolishly used to show a person's rank in society. This play was turned into a popular musical called *My Fair Lady*.

Cockney English is known for its rhyming **slang.** Here are the meanings for a few words from a cockney dictionary, or in cockney, a *dick 'n' arry*:

almond rocks – socks

apples and pears – stairs

ball and chalk – walk

boat race – face

frog and toad – road

mince pies – eyes

sky rocket – pocket

The character of Eliza Doolittle from *My Fair Lady*.

15

Changing Language

Language is constantly changing. No one knows all the reasons these changes occur, but one thing is certain—for as long as a language is spoken, it will continue to change.

The first real evidence we have of language is written language. However, oral language probably existed for thousands of years before. Our English language today is so different from the English language used between the years 500 to 1100 that reading this "Old English" is like reading a foreign language. Many of the words that we use today have been borrowed from other languages, particularly French.

*Bonjour

Ancient Writing

Sumerian word-pictures from about 3500 B.C. are the earliest known written records. Egyptian **hieroglyphics** (shown left) first appeared about 3000 B.C., written Chinese about 1500 B.C., Greek about 1400 B.C., and Latin about 500 B.C.

A Is for Alphabet

The ancient Egyptians wrote by using a system of several hundred signs that stood for whole words or for syllables. Later, people developed alphabets of individual signs which stood for particular sounds. The twenty-six-letter alphabet that writers of English use is called the Roman alphabet. It wasn't invented by the Romans though. They just added the finishing touches to a system that had been developing for thousands of years.

K	⅃	7	Phoenicians, 1000 B.C.
Λ	B	Γ	Greeks, 600 B.C.
A	B	C	Romans, A.D. 114

WORD BUILDER

A language that is no longer spoken is called a dead language. Languages that are dead include Sumerian, ancient Egyptian, Akkadian, Hittite, Etruscan, and Gothic.

P Is for Printing

Probably the greatest development in written English came in the 1400s when a printing press with movable metal type was invented. Before this time, **scribes** copied books by hand with quills. In the late 1300s, Europeans also discovered how to do wood-block printing, which the people of East Asia had been using for some time. However, it wasn't until movable type was invented that large numbers of books could be produced.

The first printing press, invented in Germany by Johannes Gutenberg, used separate metal blocks for each letter. These blocks were held together in a wooden frame to form a page. The press used a huge screw to press paper onto the inked metal blocks. Gutenberg's printing press could print about 300 pages a day.

Type blocks
Metal letter blocks were set one by one into a frame.

Paper press
A large wooden screw pressed the paper onto the inked type.

Paper bed
This held the printed paper while it dried.

Type bed
The wooden frame that held the type blocks was placed on the bed of the press.

Ink for printing
Gutenberg invented sticky, oil-based ink.

* **Dag**

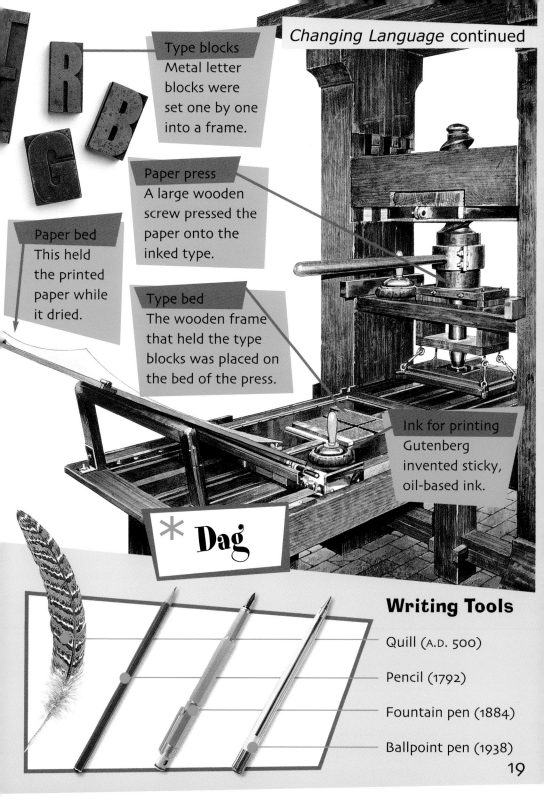

Writing Tools

Quill (A.D. 500)

Pencil (1792)

Fountain pen (1884)

Ballpoint pen (1938)

19

Look It Up!

When we don't know how to spell a word or we want to check a word's meaning, we look it up in a dictionary. The ancient Greeks and Romans were the first people to make dictionaries, but their dictionaries were usually just lists of difficult words. Today's general dictionaries include everyday words as well as difficult or technical words, listed in alphabetical order. Dictionaries may divide a word into syllables, describe how a word is pronounced and used, and explain where a word came from.

*你好

Dictionaries come in many different sizes. Some are pocket-size books. Others are so large that they're twenty **volumes**.

PROFILE

Noah Webster (1758–1843)— A Dictionary for North America

By the early 1800s, several large, fine dictionaries had been published in England. Noah Webster, an American teacher and writer, wanted to produce an equally fine dictionary of North American spellings and word usages. In 1806, Noah Webster published a small school dictionary in the United States. He then published *An American Dictionary of the English Language*, which appeared as two volumes in 1828.

Webster worked to simplify many old spellings, for example, changing the word *musick* to *music*. Since 1828, Noah Webster's American dictionaries have been updated and are widely used today.

dictionary (dik-sh6-ner-ē) *n.* a book in which words are listed alphabetically with their meanings, pronunciations, and other information. *n., plural* **dictionaries**
– ORIGIN 1500s: from medieval Latin *dictionarium*, meaning "manual or book of words"

Talk Digital

* Ciao

Language usually changes over hundreds of years, but occasionally, some huge development in society or technology speeds the process. More new words have been invented since the beginning of the computer age than at nearly any other time. Before the 1970s, a mouse was a small, furry rodent and nothing else. A chip was something you ate, and the World Wide Web was unheard of.

The development of e-mail changed language even further. The speed of e-mail encouraged people to start shortening their words and sentences. This led to a whole new style of writing. Then, when cellular phone companies brought out text messaging, language took a real leap!

FACT FINDER

How many of these text messages can you figure out? To check your answers, turn to page 31.

CUL8R

B

AFAIK

R

2U

GR8

2DAY

PLZ

THNQ

THX

B4

ATB

BFN

IDK

KIT

2NITE

XLNT

OIC

What's in a Name?

Everyone has a name, but that name does not necessarily stay the same throughout a person's life. In some cultures, people's names are changed several times as they get older. It was an Inuit practice to give newborn babies another name every time they cried, so some tiny babies had dozens of names. The Seminole tribe, in the Southeast of the United States, rewarded boys when they proved their courage in battle by giving them a new name. In many cultures, a woman may take her husband's surname when she gets married.

Choosing a name for a new baby is an important job. In many cultures, it is the parents who choose the name. The name of a Native American baby, however, is often chosen by relatives and tribal elders, not by the parents.

Inuit mother and child

This Native American baby has just been given her Indian name, War Bonnet Woman, during a naming ceremony held in her godfather's teepee.

*Shalom

These Masai tribe members from Tanzania are holding a naming ceremony. One tribe member is becoming a senior tribal elder and will be given a new name.

25

Whose Child Are You?

When people first started using family names, they often used their father's first name. In Scotland and Ireland, Mac or Mc means "son of." Now there are MacCollums, MacMillans, McArthurs and McDougals spread all over the world.

Older or Younger?

Family placement is very important in Japan, and names for **siblings** reflect this. An older sister is called *ane* and a younger sister is called *imoto*. An older brother is called *ani* and a younger brother is called *ototo*.

Happy Name Day!

As well as celebrating birthdays, people in the Czech Republic also celebrate name days, or *svátek*. Most names have their own day in the Czech calendar, for example, September 12 is the name day for people named Marie.

First Name or Family Name?

The ancient Chinese were the first people to use family names. They started this practice over 4,800 years ago. The family name was always written or spoken before the personal name.

What's Your Name?

In parts of Papua New Guinea, asking a person's name is considered impolite. If asked the names of relatives, many people will call them by their titles, such as Father or Sister, rather than by their names. They may even use a made-up name to avoid using a person's real name!

One Big Family

People in Tonga live in extended family groups. The importance of the extended family can be seen in their language. The word for siblings and cousins is the same, aunts and uncles may also be called parents, and all older people may be referred to as grandparents.

27

Fun with Words

We can have a lot of fun playing with words. One of the oldest forms of word games is the riddle. A famous riddle from ancient Greece asks this question: *What moves on four feet in the morning, two feet at noon, and sometimes three as the sun begins to go down?* The answer is a person. At the beginning, or "morning" of life, a person crawls on all fours. Throughout the "noon" of life, the person walks upright on two feet. Later in life, "as the sun begins to go down," a cane which acts as a third leg may be used.

Can you figure out the answers to these riddles?

1 What day doesn't end with the letter *y*?

2 What's the difference between a lion with a toothache and a rainy day?

3 To what question can you never answer "Yes"?

Answers: 1=Tomorrow, 2=The lion roars with pain, but the rainy day pours with rain, 3=Are you asleep?

Word Staircases

We can also have a lot of fun making patterns with words. Try making your own word staircase.

*Namaste

Step 1

Set a time limit for your game. Ten minutes should be long enough.

Step 2

Choose a letter from the alphabet. You may like to start with the first letter of your name, or simply start at the beginning of the alphabet.

Step 3

The aim is to make a staircase of words starting with your chosen letter. The first word must be a two-letter word, the second a three-letter word, and so on. The winner is the person with the most steps in a staircase when the time is up.

A								
A	N							
A	N	Y						
A	U	N	T					
A	B	O	V	E				
A	N	C	H	O	R			
A	V	E	R	A	G	E		
A	N	C	E	S	T	O	R	
A	M	E	R	I	C	A	N	A
A	M	B	A	S	S	A	D	O	R

SITESEEING · ART & ENTERTAINMENT

When did crossword puzzles begin?

Visit www.rigbyinfoquest.com

for more about LANGUAGE.

Glossary

accent – a special way of pronouncing words and phrases that is used by people from a certain area or country

dialect – a form of a language that is used only in a certain area or by a certain group of people. A dialect does not usually have a written form.

hieroglyphic – a picture of an object which stands for a word, syllable, or sound

instinctive – known naturally from birth. Some linguists believe that humans are born knowing the general principles of language.

larynx – the voice box or upper end of the windpipe containing the vocal cords

oral – spoken rather than written

scribe – a person who writes out copies of books by hand

sibling – a brother or sister

slang – words and phrases that are used in everyday speech but are not used in serious writing or formal speech

trachea – the tube that carries air between the voice box, or larynx, and the lungs. Another name for the trachea is the windpipe.

volume – one of the books of a set

Index

Fact Finder Answers

CUL8R – See you later   THX – Thanks

B – Be   B4 – Before

AFAIK – As far as I know   ATB – All the best

R – Are   BFN – Bye for now

2U – To you   IDK – I don't know

GR8 – Great   KIT – Keep in touch

2DAY – Today   2NITE – Tonight

PLZ – Please   XLNT – Excellent

THNQ – Thank you   OIC – Oh, I see

Research Starters

1 Throughout this book you will see the word *hello*, or a similar greeting, written in different languages. Research to discover which languages are in this book. Can you find other ways to say "Hello"?

2 If you could choose to learn any language in the world, which language would it be? How would you go about learning this language?

3 Do you know what your first name means? Find out the meaning behind your name, who chose it for you, and why.

4 Many of the jokes we tell are actually riddles. Find riddles from several countries or different times to share with a friend or family member.